DORSET

A portrait in colour

―――――――

HARRY ASHLEY

COUNTRYSIDE BOOKS

Also by Harry Ashley:

EXPLORE DORSET
Local Heritage Books
THE DORSET VILLAGE BOOK
Countryside Books

For Tracy who so often gets forgotten.

First Published 1986
© Harry Ashley 1986

COUNTRYSIDE BOOKS
3 CATHERINE ROAD,
NEWBURY, BERKSHIRE

ISBN 0 905392 63 9

Produced through MRM (Print Consultants) Ltd., Reading
Typeset by Acorn Bookwork, Salisbury, Wiltshire
Printed and bound in England by Woolnough Bookbinding, Wellingborough

Contents

Corfe Castle – Front Cover

A rugged ruin resting on a hilltop surrounded by battlemented towers which cling to the hillside like rotting teeth, seems an odd location for a beauty spot – yet Corfe Castle and the surrounding village is Dorset's most popular venue for tourists.

The bloody history of this defiant hillock began in a hunting lodge which preceded the castle, when Edward the Martyr King was treacherously killed by his jealous stepmother in 978 AD. Bloodshed continued during the wars of the 12th century and it was held for Matilda against King Stephen. Much cruelty and torture took place there when it was used as a prison in medieval times. The castle had its 'finest hour' during the Civil Wars. Sir John Bankes had prepared it for service to the King and it was twice besieged. The castle finally fell because of internal treachery in 1645, but the Parliamentarians could not completely destroy it with gunpowder and, over three centuries later, much of it remains to dominate a beautiful village of grey stone. During the 18th century, Corfe was the centre of the Purbeck stone industry.

Old Harry Rocks – Back Cover

Poole Bay has two natural sentinels.

Eastwards, the famous Needles and lighthouse on the Isle of Wight face the Old Harry Rocks at the tip of Ballard Down in the Purbecks, 15 miles away. A long time ago they were part of the chalk ridge which linked Dorset with the Isle of Wight. Only those who enjoy walking can reach this lonely and lovely landmark. The single pinnacle at the seaward end of the group is Old Harry, and behind him stands the Haystack. A small stump of chalk is all that remains of Old Harry's wife, which succumbed to a Channel gale at the turn of the century – incidentally, the same gale which destroyed Brighton Pier.

If you walk the half mile from Studland village, or take the longer ramble from Swanage, you will be rewarded with breathtaking views and breathe air as fresh as any in the country . . . air straight off the sea and unpolluted by the fumes from mechanical transport. The whole coastline from Studland to Hengistbury Head can be viewed, including the clifftop tower blocks which now dominate Bournemouth. To the west is the more picturesque sight of Swanage and Durlston Head.

Introduction

A group of young airmen were laughing on the shore of a small loch near Stranraer in the summer of 1944, brought together for a course of air gunnery. I was passing complimentary remarks about the countryside when a lean Scot, toughened by years of driving rivets in a Glasgow shipyard, sat upright and announced with fervour, 'This is nothing, the beauty of Scotland is contained in the Highlands. You have not lived until you have heard the drone of bagpipes drifting across a hillside at sundown.'

A diminutive 'Taffy' cut across the Scot's last words. 'It cannot equal the Llanberis Pass in North Wales where it winds around the towering mass of Mount Snowdon.' As he spoke, there was a far away look in his eyes and, for the first time, I was confronted by expressions of local pride.

Eyes turned in my direction and I knew they were expecting me to say something.

'My Dorset,' I said slowly, trying to gather my thoughts, 'is a very humble Shire County. We cannot boast of dominating mountains, or beautiful lakes, and there are no vast expanses of moorland or large forests. Dorset's variety of beauty comes in small, unexpected packages – all exciting and beautiful but with no overriding feature.'

I realised that it was an inadequate description of a beautiful coastal county and, after spending my post-war years touring the lanes and byways in search of news and pictures, I can give a more informative answer.

Dorset has been described as 'Little England' because it encompasses the attributes of many parts of England in miniature, and enables the visitor to enjoy a variety of landscapes, unspoiled by the workings and transports of heavy industry. Pilsdon Pen, for instance, one of the lovely heights down west, gave consolation to Wordsworth's sister, Dorothy, who pined for her Lakeland Hills.

Why is it a humble county? Firstly, like parts of the east coast and the west coast of Wales, it is far from industrial centres and does not attract heavy industry. Until the boundary changes in the 1970s, the county's largest town was Poole with, at that time, a population of about 70,000. Poole's greatness as a port went into recession after the prosperous days of the Newfoundland Fleets whose trade ended in the nineteenth century. Weymouth, the only other town of any size, has a steady trade with the Channel Islands but it is mainly a staging post for passengers and cargo.

County pride again came to the fore in the boundary changes. Bournemouth, internationally famous resort, and elegant Christchurch – with its proud Priory – were added to

Dorset, to the consternation of Hampshire and the towns themselves. Dorset was not happy about it either. The county of ancient boroughs did not want flamboyant Bournemouth, modern in design and progressive in projecting its image as a health resort. The merger turned out better than expected because it encouraged Poole to sharpen up, revitalise the port, attract commercial concerns wishing to move out of big cities, and project the local leisure potential. The outcome was that Poole, Bournemouth and Christchurch, with two harbours and yachting bases and miles of golden sands, could – as a unit – offer itself as a health resort second to none in the world.

Coastal leisure is the real basis of Dorset's charm.

Although the chalk hills which range from Cranborne in the north east, to Beaminster in the west form a backbone of lush farming areas, it is to the seaside that most people flock. The hills and forts of Maiden Castle, Eggarden Hill, Badbury Rings, Hambledon, Hod and Flowers Burrow are always there for those who love to walk these ancient sites, and you can climb to numerous vantage points for views of the Marshwood and Blackmoor Vales – completely unmarked by factory chimneys or signs of commercial activity. The rustic rivers, Frome and Stour, twist untidily and wildly across the county serving no other purpose than to water many mills and gurgle past the dozing anglers who come to the banks.

We have now established that the county's humbleness is based on its peaceful existence for farming, and providing leisure places for those seeking a rest from industrial stress. The county has played few major roles in the wars and uprisings that help shape a country. A king was murdered at Corfe, but that was too long ago to be of much importance and is now only a talking point for the visitors who come to Corfe and Shaftesbury, where King Edward the Martyr was finally laid to rest.

The Tolpuddle Martyrs, punished for starting one of the first trade unions and transported for their activities, are remembered in thatch in their historic village and, in Lyme Regis, you can sit on the beach where Monmouth landed in 1685. In the 20th century, a large part of the D-Day fleet, set to invade France, sailed out of Weymouth and Poole to link up in the dawn off St Aldhelm's great Head.

Humble cameos of history amuse the visitors . . . Alfred chasing a fleet of Danes which sailed over the treacherous submerged Peveril Ledge at Swanage, destroying itself. Lady Bankes, with her servants at Corfe Castle, fighting off an invading party of seamen from Poole by pouring hot ashes and boiling oil over them during the Civil Wars, and Monmouth hiding in a Dorset ditch disguised as a farm yokel, yet having in his pocket his badge of the Order of the Garter.

In the west are the villages through which Charles II fled after the Battle of Worcester, disguised as a servant, only to find that the captain of the ship which was to convey him from Charmouth was kept at home by his wife because she suspected funny business.

The ambassadors who have presented Dorset all promote the humble image. Thomas Hardy and William Barnes, the county's leading poets, were both born in small Dorset cottages and both wrote about the simple life which was their background. Later, Ralph Wightman, the famous broadcaster of the 1930s, regularly spoke to the world in the dulcet Dorset dialect, and the county's own yokel comedian, laughing Billy Burden, performs his act all over the country . . . an act projecting yokel simpleness of word and thought. He ends his performance with the catchline – 'mus' go now, 'tis a long walk back to Darset.'

Whichever part of Dorset you love most, whether it be the little that remains of Hardy's Great Heath in the east, or the lovely unspoiled hills down toward the Devon border, or sitting by the river in the so peaceful Blackmoor Vale . . . sooner or later you will find your way to the sea, and what a magic choice there is.

The children love the sandy beaches of Bournemouth and Weymouth, and there are the hills of Purbeck rolling off the sea like giant Channel waves, and the bleak Isle of Portland from whose interior came the stone which graces many famous buildings all over the world. Some like the cruel trap of pebbles which form Chesil Beach – the last resting place of many a fine ship swept ashore by Channel westerlies, and the romantic choose Lyme Regis at the County's border with Devon. All along this seaboard are the locations which inspired authors and poets.

At Mudeford, Coleridge and Sir Walter Scott found inspiration on the sandy spit which overlooks the ancient Hengistbury Head. In a house on the Bournemouth clifftop Robert Louis Stevenson penned his *Kidnapped* and *Dr Jekyll and Mr Hyde*. Keats spent his last night in England on a boat off Lulworth Cove, and Rupert Brook sought solitude there many years later. The chill clifftops along the Purbeck range inspired Hardy and Llewellin Powys, and a shipwreck off St Aldhelms Head was the basis for a Dickens story. The loss of the *Halswell* with over 150 lives, features in the author's *Long Journey*. Meade Faulkner chose Fleet and the Chesil beach for his thrilling *Moonfleet* and, in Lyme Regis, they will not let you forget that Jane Austen favoured the resort, and the ancient Cobb features in her works.

Dorset has countless fine houses and gardens open to the public and, in keeping with the county's humble image, they display themselves with dignity. You will find no zoos or funfairs to attract you. Such historic places as Forde Abbey, Athelhampton Hall, Sherborne Castle and Wolveton Hall welcome you.

Amongst the great floral displays are the Botanical Gardens at Abbotsbury, and Minterne Magna where the Digby family – authorities on rhododendrons – open their gardens each year.

I have refrained from telling of my favourite corners of Dorset Dear. It is better that I leave the last word to rural poet, William Barnes, who says it all in his poem *In Praise of Dorset*.

We Do'set, though we mid be hwomely,
  Be'nt ashëamed to own our pleäce;
An' we've zome women not uncomely;
  Nor ashëamed to show their feäce;
We've a meäd or two wo'th mowèn,
We've an ox or two wo'th showèn,
    In the village,
    At the tillage.
Come along an' you shall vind
That Do'set men don't sheame their kind.
  Friend an' wife,
  Fathers, mothers, sisters, brothers,
  Happy, happy, be their life!
  Vor Do'set dear,
  Then gi'e woone cheer;
  D'ye hear? woone cheer!

If you in Do'set be a roamèn,
  An' ha' business at a farm,
Then woont ye zee your eale a foamèn!
  Or your cider down to warm?
Woont ye have brown bread a-put ye,
An' some vinny cheese a-cut ye?
    Butter? – rolls o't!
    Cream? – why bowls o't!

Woont ye have, in short, your vill,
A-gi'ed wi' a right good will?
  Friend an' wife,
  Fathers, mothers, sisters, brothers,
  Happy, happy, be their life!
  Vor Do'set dear,
  Then gi'e woone cheer;
  D'ye hear? woone cheer!

An woont ye have vor ev'ry shillèn,
  Shillen's wo'th at any shop.
Though Do'set chaps be up to zellèn
  An' can meäke a tidy swop?
Use 'em well, they'll use you better;
In good turns they woont be debtor.
    An' so comely,
    An' so hwomely,
Be the maidens, if your son
Took woone o'm, then you'd cry 'Well done!'
  Friend an' wife,
  Fathers, mothers, sisters, brothers,
  Happy, happy, be their life!
  Vor Do'set dear,
  Then gi'e woone cheer;
  D'ye hear? woone cheer!

The Old Custom House, Poole

Christchurch

When King Alfred of Wessex set up a series of fortified towns called burghs as a protection against Danish invaders, Christchurch, or as it was known then Tweoxneam or Twyneham, was one of them. That was 1100 years ago, and the castle set on a mound on the spit of land formed by the meeting of the Dorset river Stour and the Hampshire Avon, is now a ruin. But the magnificent Norman Priory with a dominating 15th century tower 120 feet high overlooks the two rivers. In summer they are crowded with yachts and cruisers and nosey swans paddling amongst the moorings waiting for titbits. Here in the cold winter sunlight, cruisers on the Avon are seen cloaked in protective awnings.

The town takes its name from a legend concerning Christ the Carpenter. The church was to be built on St Catherine's Hill a mile away, but each night material taken to the hilltop was mysteriously moved back to the church's present site. The builders thought it must be divine guidance and started to build on the spit. A mysterious workman joined them in the task but never came to the meal table. One day a beam cut too short was left overnight. Next day the beam was found not only in place, but overlong. The workman was never seen again and the masons were convinced that he was the Carpenter of Nazareth.

You do not have to believe this story but the beam is still on show though not in its original position.

Shicsack Day is on May 29th. At Ower children wear oakapples and the more pugnacious fight each other after argument repeating:
Shicsack, Shicsack,
Lousy back, lousy back.

Hengistbury Head

The great land mass at the eastern end of the Bournemouth coast has a long history – in contrast to 150 odd years existence of the popular resort. But most visitors who climb to the heights for views of the Solent and Isle of Wight have little knowledge of the Head's antiquity.

The legend that it was named after Hengist and that he was buried there has been destroyed by historians. The German mercenary never got that far west. The late Pat Palmer in *What's In A Name* connects this holidaymaker's paradise with the Norse sea-king Heddin who fled from Norway with the daughter of one of his enemies. At that time its name was Hednesburia. It became known as Hynesbury in Stuart times, and Hengistbury is a corruption of this. It was a stronghold in prehistoric times and eleven thousand years ago men hunted reindeer there.

The Double Dykes, built in the Iron Age as a defence on the shoreward side of the peninsula, are still in existence and coins have been found made in a British mint before the Romans came. Near the tip of the headland are deep excavations where iron orestone was extracted and conveyed by barges to Bucklers Hard where it was used for shipbuilding.

It was thought that Napoleon would attempt an invasion and land near Hengistbury, so a battery was established. But his fleet luckily was destroyed at Trafalgar. Today a little 'Noddy' train conveys visitors to and from the sandy beach on Mudeford Spit.

Lay things by and they will come to use.
Dorset motto

Bournemouth Pier

Bournemouth has a sand cliff seaboard but the East and West Cliffs drop down to sea level at the valley of the Bourne Stream. Elegant lawns and gardens line the banks of this stream which enters the sea at the Pier Approach, in a rather undignified fashion through a concrete conduit. Bournemouth has had several piers and the Approach several new faces. This – the latest – houses restaurants and pleasure pavilions. A flyover bridge takes traffic over the tip of the Approach, leaving it clear for the hordes of holidaymakers who make this their quickest route to the sea.

Missing in this modern picture are the popular paddle steamers which once sailed from the pierhead even as far as Cherbourg, and the donkey drawn bathchairs which made Bournemouth famous. They once waited at the Approach like taxis, taking elderly fares for a ride along the promenade.

If the Abbess were to marry the Abbot of
 Glastonbury,
Their heir would have more land than the King
 of England.
At Shaftesbury

Bournemouth Autumn

The Bournemouth War Memorial stands between a locked daffodil garden called Paradise and the noisier area of tennis courts on the banks of the Bourne in the Upper Gardens. It is best seen in autumn when the russet-coloured leaves carpet the green lawns.

Following the course of the little Bourne makes a pleasant walk in this garden 'city'. The visitor can follow it for over a mile and beyond the Bournemouth boundary, until it disappears unceremoniously into a conduit beneath the railway bank at Branksome. As its course is followed inland, so the gardens become simpler and more natural in layout. The familiar pink blossom trees give way to tall poplars and shady weeping willows.

Near the Poole border, the waters of Coy Pond – a little bird sanctuary, – join the Bourne as it gurgles over little falls all the way to the sea.

We are turning yellow, master,
And next we are turning red,
And faster then and faster
Shall seek our rooty bed,
All wasted in disaster.
But you lift not your head.
Thomas Hardy

Poole Guildhall

Much of old Poole, including some of the fine merchants' houses, has been preserved including the Guildhall of 1761. It was the gift of the town's MPs and, like the Custom House on the nearby quay, has two semicircular sets of steps leading to an ornate Tuscan porch. It served its purpose until a new Municipal Building was built in 1932. Now it is one of the town's three Municipal Museums, all housed in buildings of historical interest. Matters maritime can be seen in the Town Cellars on the quay, and ancient Scaplens Court is just around the corner. Both are 15th century buildings.

Poole and Bournemouth have grown up on what was once great tracts of heathland which gave the smugglers both good vantage points and cover. Both towns have retained their coastal parts as salubrious residential areas and, in each case, mass estates form a suburbia further inland.

Who's A-fear'd?
On the cap badge of the old Dorset Regt.

Poole Quay

When trading vessels could no longer make the port of Wareham because of silting and the fact that the vessels were larger, Poole became the principal port in the harbour. The change took place at the end of the 12th century and Poole and Wareham have been 'feuding' ever since. In 1364 the Barons of Winchelsea issued a certificate confirming Poole's sea boundaries, and fishing limits within the harbour. At frequent intervals the Mayor of Poole, who is also Admiral of the Port, 'Beats the Bounds' in a colourful procession attended by scores of little craft and pirate gangs. In the 17th century the harbour was prosperous and sometimes full of the ships engaged in the Newfoundland fishing trade. By the end of the 19th century, Poole had amassed a fleet of nearly 300 ships and the harbour often resembled a forest with the tall masts of the great sailing ships darkening the sky.

Today most of the commercial shipping, in the form of cross-Channel ferries, sails from Hamworthy and the old Town Quay, with its 18th century warehouses and old inns, is often lined with pleasure craft. A 20th century replica of Drake's *Golden Hind* dominates in this photograph.

Tis not because this womans virtue dies
That the brass tells us here Ann Hillary lies:
Her name's long lov'd, she is in this commended
The poor cry out their Hillary Term is ended.
Brass plate to Ann Hillary in
Canford Church 1653

Poole Harbour – Sunset Over Brownsea

Magnificent sunsets are a feature of Poole's vast waterway, one of the largest natural harbours in the world. From this location, aptly named Evening Hill, the celebrated painter J. M. W. Turner was so inspired that he painted a sunset picture.

The vantage point on the Sandbanks road is the best place to view the harbour with its 90 miles of coastline, 28 square miles of water and 8 named islands. Brownsea, the largest of these, is in the background of the photograph. The view from Evening Hill also encompasses Old Harry Rocks in the Purbecks and Corfe Castle looking diminutive against the larger hills in the Purbeck range.

Here under this syone
Lie Ruth and old John
Who smoked all his life
And so did his wife;
And now ther's no doubt
But their pipes are both out.
Be it said without joke
That life is but smoke,
Though you live to four score,
'Tis a whiff and no more.
Of Rector John Warren of
Marnhull 1752

22

Compton Acres

Compton Acres' magnificent gardens were created out of savage moorland on western facing slopes at Canford Cliffs overlooking Poole Harbour.

Thomas Simpson laid out the gardens just after the First World War on land that had been a wilderness of gorse and heather. The series of gardens were designed so that none overlooked another. The construction took several years and cost £220,000. Tons of stone and topsoil were imported and, for the Japanese garden, a shipload of plants, bushes and flowers were brought to Poole from the East . . . and the Japanese gardeners came with them.

Bronze and other statuary, and wellheads, some museum pieces, were collected from all over the world.

Two other owners have added to Mr Simpson's work, but in 1986 a new owner decided to demolish the 1914 built house which is part of the Gardens.

Many thousands of visitors annually step across these stones, part of the Japanese garden.

Sweet garden! peaceful spot! no more in thee
Shall I e'er while away the sunny hour.
Farewell each blooming shrub and lofty tree;
Farewell the mossy path and nodding flower!
I shall not hear again from yonder bower
The song of birds or humming of the bee,
Nor listen to the waterfall, nor see
The clouds float on behind the lofty tower.
No more, at breezy eve, or dewy morn,
My gliding scythe shall sheer the mossy green;
My busy hands shall never more adorn.
My eyes no more may see, this peaceful scene,
But still, sweet spot, wherever I may be,
My love-led soul will wander back to thee.
William Barnes

Poole Bay

Poole Bay has long been favoured as a venue for yachting. Its proximity to the Isle of Wight causes four weak tides a day, so competitors in international events are not disadvantaged by any strong tide conditions which would favour local competitors with knowledge of such conditions. Many world class events are staged with clubs from Poole Harbour acting as hosts and organisers.

The racing fleets speeding across the Bay with their multi-coloured spinnakers billowing, and turning at the marker buoys offshore, provide entertainment for the visitors on the Poole and Bournemouth beaches.

In the picture J24s sail the blue waters of the Bay with the cliffs of Bournemouth in the distant background.

I often have been beate and bandge:
My friends rejoice to see me handge:
And when my friends doe chance to die
Then I aloud for them will cry.
Written in the belltower of Okeford
Fitzpaine Church in 1658

Swanage – Mill Pond

A man with a Dick Whittington lifestyle is responsible for making Swanage an architectural museum. Poor boy, John Mowlem, begged a ship's captain carrying Purbeck stone, for a passage to London town. He made a fortune, paving many of London's famous streets with marble.

Later, his own ships returning to Swanage brought strange cargoes from buildings he had demolished in old London as ballast. A faceless clock tower, which once stood as a memorial to Wellington on London Bridge, was removed as a traffic hazard. John Mowlem erected it on the shores of Swanage Bay. The Town Hall has a facade which was originally the front of the Mercers Hall in Cheapside. Other finds decorate Purbeck House in the High Street and Durlston Castle. Until recent years, the promenade was lit from lamp standards which once graced Soho and St Martin in the Fields.

The same John Mowlem gave Swanage its most photographed beauty spot. The Mill Pond, built into the side of a hill and surrounded by cottages of local stone, is portrayed here.

Swanage has retained all the charm of a Victorian resort. The small promenade nestles in the lee of the chalk cliffs and Peveril Point. It was on the ledge off Peveril that the Danish fleet perished when fleeing from King Alfred, and a monument on the seafront commemorates the victory. Amusingly, it is topped with four cannonballs but the battle took place many years before gunpowder was invented.

Oak before Ash
Only be a splash.
A Dry Summer

Ringstead and Whitenose

Between Lulworth and Weymouth is a little known stretch of beach called Ringstead Bay. A narrow road leads off the main A353 near Poxwell and twists for two miles to Ringstead, which is a small hamlet of a few dwellings. The fields reach right down to the beach. Yet this small inaccessible part of Dorset is mentioned in the Domesday Book, but much of it was destroyed by pirates and the church has vanished.

Today the artists come and set up their easels to commit the nearby Whitenose cliff on to canvas. The great Nose reaches out into Weymouth Bay looking like a rugged sheepdog lying with its head on its paws. It is a friendly peaceful place but was not always so. The 18th-century smugglers operated from this beach and lit gorse fires on the slopes of the cliffs to warn their ships at sea of the presence of contraband officers and to stay offshore.

Since man to man has been so unjust
I cannot tell what man to trust.
I trust so many to my sorrow,
Pay today and trust tomorrow.
William Mabey, signwriter

Durdle Door

Of all of Dorset's beautiful and varied coast, the stretch from Worbarrow Bay to Osmington is supreme. Whitenose, Swyre Head, Durdle Door, Lulworth and Mupe Bay are contained in this area.

Here, bathed in warm evening sunshine, the cliffs at Durdle Door adopt grandiose golden hues. Green fields, rugged chalk cliffs and pebble beaches continue into the background and, in the far distance standing on the horizon, the eastern extremity, St Aldhelm's head. The Dorset Coast Walk leads you uphill and down dale along these beautiful Dorset cliffs.

No wonder Do'set volk can rise to fame,
For Do'set's sons and daughters justly claim
That other hills no greater glories show
Than Pilsden, Lewesdon, Batcombe, Bulbarrow.

Weymouth

Weymouth takes its name from the river Wey but most of the known resort is actually Melcome Regis on the east bank of the river. A very royal town because it was not only the favourite resort of George III, but it was here that he did a magnificent public relations job by popularising bathing as a health cure. His ornate stone statue, now gaudily painted, stands where the main streets meet the esplanade. Guarded by a lion and a unicorn, he surveys the grand Georgian terraces which house the visitors who for generations have followed the King's example.

Queen Victoria is also well represented. Her statue faces the King but at the northern end of the promenade. Midway between them is the colourful and ornate Jubilee Clock which commemorates the Queen's Golden Jubilee, and has frequently been used by lovers as a meeting point.

Weymouth proper across the Town Bridge is mainly residential except for the Nothe gardens and fort at the seaward end.

The grand old High Street was practically obliterated by a German landmine in the last war, and only the 18th century Town Hall and the Boot Inn escaped without damage. Overlooking the Portland Harbour is a ruined blockhouse built by Henry VIII. Sandsfoot Castle is crumbling into the sea.

When we lay where Budmouth Beach is,
O, the girls were fresh as peaches,
With their tall and tossing figures and their eyes
    of blue and brown!
And our hearts would ache with longing
as we paced from our sing-songing,
With a smart Clink! Clink! up the esplanade
    and down.
                              Thomas Hardy

Pulpit Rock

This strange rock formation on the southernmost tip of the island of Portland is known as Pulpit Rock because, with a little assistance from Man in placing a linking slab with toe holes to bridge the gap, it resembles a church pulpit. It faces down-Channel and withstands the full force of the gales that sweep up from the west, across Deadman's Bay.

This rock table is the scene of countless wrecks. Sailing ships, yachts, and even the old paddle steamer *Bournemouth* ended their days at the foot of it. Yet like that other cruel place, Corfe Castle, it is a favourite spot for visitors who only see it on sunny summer days.

If it thunders on All Fool's Day
It brings good crops of corn and hay.
April 1st

Chesil Beach

Local old salts will tell you that the phenomenon of pebble which links Portland to the mainland came up in a night, but scientifically we know that the pebbles gather here from many parts of the coast and stand on a foundation of Kimmeridge clay. They get smaller and smaller as the beach reaches west for ten miles to Abbotsbury and, by the time it reaches Bridport, becomes fine shingle. It is said that fishermen coming ashore in a fog or at night can tell where they are by the size of the pebbles. At Portland the bank is 40 feet high and 600 feet wide at its base.

The great barrier faces the Channel storms. Officially called West Bay, it was more aptly named Deadman's Bay by Thomas Hardy and, in fact, the seabed is strewn with thousands of wrecks. Several ships have been washed ashore at the doorstep of the Cove Inn, seen in the photograph, which is the eastern extremity of the Chesil Beach.

The glowering cliffs behind are the heights of East Weare and, on the extreme right, is Blacknor Point. The 20,000 ton liner, *Winchester Castle*, ran ashore here in 1936 in a dense fog. It was an unhappy last passage for the captain. Two miles from Portland a strip of water trapped between the beach and the mainland is known as the Fleet. It extends as far as Abbotsbury where it is part of the famous swannery.

> In the wild October nightime, when the wind
> raved round the land,
> And the Back-sea met the Front-sea, and our
> doors were blocked with sand,
> And we heard the drum of Dead-man's Bay,
> where bones of thousands are,
> We knew not what the day had done for
> us at Trafalgar.
>
> *Thomas Hardy*

Old Cottages – Portland

The Portland stone, which so elegantly decorates famous buildings, is used in a more functional manner on the island to build the cottage homes. Most of them have a traditional stone porch as the only decoration on plain block residences, and these protect callers from the cruel winds which sweep the island.

This row at Wakeham would be more in keeping on a Mediterranean island. Some are enhanced by 20th century colour washes but the building on the extreme right, still sporting an ancient thatched roof, is Avice's Cottage which features in Thomas Hardy's 'The Well Beloved', and is now the Portland Museum. In the grounds of this museum, which stands on the slopes leading to Church Ope Cove, are rare Portland Blackfaced Sheep. Once the islanders lived by fishing and farming and Portland Mutton was a delicacy but, like Dorset's famous Blue Vinny cheese, it is now a legendary dish.

Portland, a great mass of oolite rock, shaped like a bird's beak, is 496 feet high at its highest point and slowly slopes down to the sea where, at Portland Bill, it is only 20 feet above the sea. Four and a half miles long, it is only two miles wide.

The bleak Victorian prison, now a Borstal Institution, was originally built to provide labour for lumping the stone for the breakwaters forming Portland's man-made harbour.

If Candlemas Day be fair and fine,
Half the Winter's left behind.
If Candlemas Fair be wind and storm,
Half the Winters still to come.
Candlemas Fair February 2nd

Portland Bill Lighthouse

Treeless and colourless with inhospitable shores, Portland attracts visitors because it is one of the most interesting venues along the whole of the south coast. This island from whose bowels the stone was quarried which enhances famous buildings all over the world, is left scarred by centuries of digging since Inigo Jones discovered the worth of the stone as an elegant building material in the 17th century. It adorns famous buildings all over London. St Paul's Cathedral and Buckingham Palace were decorated with it and the Cenotaph in Whitehall was dug out of a small quarry near the Portland Museum. Unsuitable squares of the stone are discarded and scattered over the island like giant toy bricks. The loom of the lighthouse warns shipping not only of the cruel rocks, but of the Race just off the island where several tides meet and the sea is always in turmoil. This Race has whirlpooled many a fine ship to a watery grave. Nearby on the notorious Shambles Sandbank, the *Abergavenny* — commanded by poet Wordsworth's brother — went down in 1805, with the loss of 300 lives.

Portland Bill, like Lulworth Cove, is one of the nation's beauty spots but, analogous with Lulworth, its beauty has been marred by enormous car parks. Having lobster teas and Portland doughcake in one of the little wooden shacks which serve as restaurants, is one of the remembered pleasures of generations who love this remote tip of Dorset.

Who rings a bell
Let him look well
To hand and head and Heart –
To hand for work, To head for skill,
The hearts for worships part.
Edgar F. Cull. In the ringing
chamber of Lillington Church

White Horse

Most prominent of all the white horses cut into the south's chalk hills is the equestrian figure of George III, which is visible to visitors all along Weymouth's seafront. Intended as a token of gratitude and loyalty because the Monarch had brought much prosperity to the town, the burgesses were aghast when they saw that George had been portrayed leaving instead of arriving. A legendary tale says that the artist, overwrought at what he had done, committed suicide by throwing himself over the cliff.

As is so often true, the facts are less interesting. The horse and rider were cut into the hillside above Osmington in 1807 to the order of one John Ranier, under the supervision of a Mr Wood – a local bookseller. It is possible that the King was purposely portrayed going in an easterly direction because he was going to visit his friend, Sir Thomas Weld, at Lulworth Castle.

The image is two hundred and fifty feet high and three hundred feet wide, the horse's tail is as wide as a street, and climbing over the horse is an early adventure for most Weymouth schoolboys.

Dorset's other figure cut into the chalk is at Cerne Abbas. The famous giant, displaying all in his nakedness, is much older than the White Horse and is thought to have been carved long before the Romans came. The giant is 180 feet high with 7 foot long fingers, and he holds a club 120 feet long.

Where simple nature reigns, and every view
Diffusive, spreads the pure Dorsetian Downs
In boundless prospect.
Thomson on Eastbury

Abbotsbury

There is no need to come to Abbotsbury except to enjoy its beauty and famous gardens and Swannery. Other roads will lead westward far more quickly but, on arrival, the feeling that you are treading on holy ground causes you to speak in whispers. Once a railway conveyed visitors on a single track line from Upwey. That disappeared with the Beeching rail cuts.

Nine centuries ago, Orca, senechal to Canute, built an Abbey here, peopled by monks from Cerne. It dominated the village for 500 years and, when the Abbey was destroyed during the Dissolution of the Monasteries, the great barn remained almost intact. It has the grace of a cathedral, with a doorway befitting a palace. Little else of the Abbey remains except a gateway to the old vicarage and odd stones, built into modern dwellings.

The church was the centre of a battle in the Civil Wars when Cavaliers sniped at Roundheads from the tower. The pulpit still bears shot holes made by Cromwell's men. A fierce battle for the Abbey House ended in its destruction.

The Swannery was established 600 years ago, in the flat water behind Chesil Beach, to provide meat for the monks. Today, it is a bird sanctuary. On a hilltop above the village stands St Catherine's Chapel, built completely of stone. The ancient place of worship has withstood 400 years of westerly gales and was a landmark for sailors coming up-Channel. An Iron Age fort on another hilltop is worth visiting – a place giving fine views of the Channel and Portland.

The Frome wi' ever water'd brink
Do run where shelven hills do Zink.
William Barnes on the river Frome

Golden Cap

The variety of coastline along the Dorset shore is one of its unique features. Pebbles, sand and chalk cliffs are in abundance. But in the far west is what is known as the fossil coast — black muddy unstable cliffs which contain countless fossils. Schoolchildren come in organised parties each year hoping to emulate 12 year old Mary Anning who, in 1811, discovered in the cliff-face what was later identified as an ichthyosaurus. It is now housed in the London Natural History Museum.

Dominating this piece of coast with such uninviting names as the Black Ven and Spittles, is one crowning glory . . . Golden Cap, 617 feet above the sea, just west of the little coastal village of Seatown. In sunlight its top glistens like gold, and it is worth the climb after refreshment at the little inn seen in the foreground.

There are some heights in Wessex, as if by
    kindly hand
For thinking, dreaming, dyingon, and at crises
    when I stand,
Say, on Ingpen Beacon eastward, or on
    Wylls-Neck westwardly,
I seem where I was before my birth, and
    after my death may be.
                 Thomas Hardy

The Cobb, Lyme Regis

Do not come to Lyme Regis if you are in a hurry, because this lovely little place of narrow streets and lanes wandering aimlessly beside waters which tumble down the hillside to the sea, does not wish to know about town planning – neither does it recognise the needs of motorists to be of prime importance.

Come to Lyme and enjoy a resort that likes to be old fashioned, a town which has inspired authors, a town which is one of the oldest 'Loyal and Ancient Boroughs' in Britain with known roots as far back as 755 AD, when Kenwulf was king of the West Saxons.

To protect a fishing fleet on this exposed Channel shore, the 800 feet long Cobb was built during the reign of Edward I. It was also conveniently placed for vessels engaged in continental trade. Thought to be one of the earliest artificial harbours, it is a curving breakwater which offers shelter on both sides.

In the Civil War, the brave folk of Lyme – defending the town for Parliament – held off an attack by 4,000 Royalists, and it was on a beach adjacent to the Cobb that Monmouth landed to start his ill-fated rebellion against James II in 1685.

As a princess, Queen Victoria sailed from an arm of the Cobb which now bears her name.

Jane Austen used the Cobb as a location in her last great novel *Persuasion*, and Tennyson came to Lyme to see this spot where the fictitious Louisa Musgrove fell. More recently, author John Fowles, who is also honorary curator of the town's museum, featured the Cobb in the film version of his novel *The French Lieutenant's Woman*.

Today it is mainly yachts and fishing boats which moor in the shelter of the Cobb, here seen on a cold winter morning at low tide.

It is a sturdy work, laid down on mysterious lines and bearing a resemblance to no marine structure of like intent. It wanders into the water in a hesitating manner.
Sir Frederick Treves on the Cobb at Lyme

Dorchester

Dorchester, county town of Dorset and centred in the heart of lush farming country on the banks of the Frome. The river skirts the shopping centre, hiding itself behind the gaunt prison, and re-emerges where the main street gives way to open fields on the Bournemouth road going east.

It has changed little over the years with statues of its two literary giants watching over the passing traffic. Thomas Hardy sits comfortably on a plinth at the top of High West Street, and William Barnes, in bronze, stands beneath the tower of St Peter's Church – seen in background. Both had many connections with the town, and Barnes first saw his beloved Julia jump down off a stagecoach outside the Kings Arms Hotel, and vowed to marry her.

The ancient Assize Courts, no longer used by law, are preserved as a memorial to the Six Men of Dorset, the Tolpuddle Martyrs, who were transported for collectively protesting about their low wage levels in 1834.

In the Antelope Hotel is the room where the notorious Judge Jeffreys held his 'Bloody Assizes' after Monmouth's rebellion. The Judge's lodgings, a 17th century house opposite St Peter's Church, is now a restaurant. The town, of course, is much older. It dates back to the Iron Age, and in 70 AD the Romans founded their Durnovaria on the banks of the Frome.

An earthwork constructed about 2000 BC was a sacred circle. The Romans improved it and made it into an amphitheatre where gladiators fought and, in the 18th century, it was used as a place of public execution. Maumbury Rings today is a peaceful open space where children come to play and dogs are exercised.

A doctor could neither live nor die there.
Dorset saying about Dorchester

Maiden Castle

A visit to Maiden Castle can be a traumatic experience because this hill fort, with a history going back to 3000 BC, does not have crowds of visitors and you may find yourself alone with countless ghosts. Two miles south of Dorchester, the castle on view today dates from the first century BC. Excavations have proved that under the eastern end a Neolithic village once existed.

About 1800 BC the hilltop became deserted until the 5th or 4th century BC, when the existing earthworks were built.

It became an Iron Age Hill Fort and spread west with suburbs encircled by an extension of the rampart.

It was one of the finest earthworks in Britain following new methods of fortification around 100 BC. The defences enclosed 47 acres and, in its prime, 5,000 people lived here tilling the land and keeping sheep and cattle.

The Roman General, Vespasian, and his 2nd Legion arrived in 44 AD, overwhelmed the resident tribes and used the fort as a temporary military outpost until they moved down the slopes to establish the Roman settlement at Dorchester.

This place, which was home to Celts and a fort for Romans, became disused in the 5th century AD. So perhaps it is natural that if you wander across this ancient sward on a winter's day when the west wind whistles through the ramparts, you will find it awesome. Thomas Hardy called it a 'stupendous ruin'.

The hills talk together and the listening valleys hear
All our eyes are turned to the bright pavillions.
Sir Hugh Walpole quoting Blake
when travelling from Salisbury through
the Blackmoor Vale

Hardy's Monument

From their early days the people who live at Weymouth are aware of the little monument on the range of hills which separates the resort and Dorchester, but many of them still believe that it commemorates Thomas Hardy. They forget the county's other Hardy, Sir Thomas Masterman Hardy, in whose arms Lord Nelson died at Trafalgar.

Erected in 1884, it was designed by Arthur Dyke Ackland-Troyte. A crinoline style base supports a 70 foot octagonal tower with a bulging top. Its door is locked and you cannot go to the top – not that it matters because the hilltop here is 777 feet above the sea and provides a viewpoint to enjoy some of the finest scenery in Dorset. Seaward the view takes you beyond Weymouth Bay and Portland's great harbour to the island itself, wallowing in the water like a massive sleeping whale. Behind you is a patchwork of Dorset farmland.

Now you have taken the trouble to come to these heights, other interesting sites are at hand. A few hundred yards south of the monument is the Hellstone, a Neolithic dolmen standing at the entrance to a chambered long barrow. This burial place was erected about 4000 BC but was incorrectly rebuilt in 1866. Nearer Portesham are two sets of ancient stones . . . the Valley of Stones and the Grey Mare and Colts.

A stone seat at the foot of Hardy's Monument commemorates Lt-Col. Digby Oswald DSO who died on the Somme in 1916.

Apples fine
And the cider wrung to year will be as wine.
Thomas Hardy

Hardy's Cottage

At Higher Bockhampton, near Dorchester, devotees of Thomas Hardy come in thousands to visit the author's humble birthplace. It is slowly being encroached upon and cosseted by the forest he so often wrote about.

The simple thatched cottage was built by his grandfather, and Hardy fans will know that in the central upstairs room, where the poet was born, a doctor cast him aside proclaiming him dead. A nurse picked up the baby, 'Stop a minute, he's alive sure enough', she said, and her action saved the life of one of England's greatest authors.

Sitting in the window of the adjoining room, he later wrote *Under the Greenwood Tree*.

At nearby Stinsford, the Mellstock of his novels, Hardy's family used to worship at the little church, and it is fitting that his heart should be buried there with his first wife beneath a shady tree.

The National Trust take care of the famous cottage and, to save wear and tear, only visitors with written permits can enter the building.

Hardy not only used Dorset and its people as background for his works, but renamed much of the county in his fictional Wessex. This was a literary ploy which enabled him to write about real people and places. Dorchester was his Casterbridge, Weymouth and Bournemouth became Budmouth and Sandbourne, and Portland was the Isle of Slingers.

cum wind, cum weather
Darzet volk 'ull stick together
Rhoda Moore

Tolpuddle

The violent picket line battles between striking trade unionists and the police are a far cry from the peaceful village of Tolpuddle, but strangely enough trade unionism had its early roots on the little shady green at the centre of this single street village.

In 1831, six farm labourers met beneath a sycamore tree and made a pact which was probably the beginning of trade unionism. They were men of strong Christian beliefs and were not even asking for more pay. They only wanted their bosses to stop reducing their wages which had dropped from nine shillings to seven shillings in three years. It was the last straw for them when the authorities decided to cut another shilling off their already meagre pittance. The Friendly Society of Agricultural Workers was formed in the village and very soon the leader, George Loveless, a staunch Wesleyan local preacher, and five others were also arrested.

They were sentenced to transportation, not for what they had done, but in order to make an example of them. There was a public outcry and a petition of 800,000 signatures was sent to Parliament. They all eventually received a free pardon.

The village has never forgotten the Six Men of Dorset. Not only is there a memorial seat on the green, but a row of six memorial cottages centred around a small museum.

My Lord, if we have violated any law, it was not done intentionally; we have injured no man's character, reputation, person or property; we are uniting together to preserve ourselves, our wives and our children from utter degradation and starvation.

George Loveless, Tolpuddle Martyr. His defence at the trial of the Six Men of Dorset, 1834

Gold Hill, Shaftesbury

As if it was not famous enough, Gold Hill at Shaftesbury has received modern fame in television advertising. The small lad in tattered cap pushing his bicycle loaded with bread has earned the cobbled street the new name of 'Hovis Hill'.

This view of the simple thatched cottages, and the great buttresses of the retaining wall on the right, has satisfied generations of artists and photographers. In the background, the Blackmoor Vale is a patchwork of trees and farmland. A quaint pretty town where through traffic is cleverly bypassed, in spite of the fact that it stands on a hilltop.

Shaftesbury, which once boasted a castle, three mints, an abbey, twelve churches and hospitals on this 700 foot high hill, has also lost its four market crosses. The ancient town's finest hour came on the 20th February 979 AD when King Edward, murdered at Corfe Castle, was brought here to his final resting place.

The museum is housed in a building that was once a dosshouse to accommodate travelling men from fairs and markets.

While Paladore, on watch, do strain
Her eyes to Blackmwore's blue-hilled plain,
While Duncliffe is the travellers mark,
Or cloty Stour a-rollen dark;
Or while our bells do call, for greace,
The vo'k avore their Savior's feace,
Mid Paladore an' Poll a dear,
Vor ever know
O' peace an' plenty down below.
William Barnes

Milton Abbas

Milton Abbas was once a thriving market town surrounding the Abbey. It had many streets and the historian Treves tells us that it had a grammar school founded in 1521, over a hundred houses, many taverns and a 'brewery of great renown'. The extreme possessiveness of the Earl of Dorchester in the 18th century ended all that. He wanted to build his mansion near the Abbey and with high handedness, typical of many 18th century squires, razed the town to the ground and rebuilt Milton Abbas as a model village, just over the hill and out of his sight. Sir William Chambers built the village in 1780, his plan chosen in preference to one submitted by Capability Brown.

Encompassed in a fold in the chalk hills, the single street village can be approached from the heights of Bulbarrow or from the Puddletown to Blandford road (A354) turning left at Milbourne St Andrew.

In this early attempt at town planning, sturdy thatched cottages were built on each side of the wide road. Each had an expanse of lawn at the front and, between them, a great chestnut tree. Alas, the trees became diseased a few years ago and were cut down, thus spoiling the full beauty of the planning. An inn, and a church by James Wyatt are included in the complex, as well as neat almshouses.

Milton Abbey, on the original site, was built over two hundred years – between 1322 and 1539. The mansion was built in 1771 around a quadrangle which makes it perfect for its present use as a school. When you walk across the lawns, and you can in school holidays, remember that once this was a busy town.

O blessed St Catherine lend me thine aid,
And grant that I never die an old maid.
The Shrine of St Catherine, Milton Abbas

Ashmore Bluebells

Persistent plucking by generations of children has seriously diminished our bluebell woods, but here near Ashmore, in the centre of the great Cranborne Chase, the pretty flowers grow profusely in and around such woodland as Stubhampton Bottom, which is still in its primeval state.

Here on the hilltop above Farnham, clusters of bluebells form carpets around the ancient trees. In the valley below, you get glimpses of the patchwork of green and gold fields and the occasional bright yellow of oil seed rape. Beyond is the Dorset Cursus, that processional way from Neolithic times, so old yet we can trace its course from Gussage St Michael to Bokerly Dyke on the Dorset border near Pentridge.

No city primness train'd my feet
To strut in childhood through the street,
But freedom let them loose to tread
The yellow cowslips' downcast head;
Or climb, above the twining hop
And ivy, to the elm trees' top;
Where southern airs of blue-sky'd day
Breath'd oe'r the daisy and the may.
I knew you young, and love you now,
O shining grass, and shady bough.
William Barnes

Blandford

This Dorset market town has the unique distinction of having all its main central buildings built in the same period.

The town was practically razed to the ground in 1731 but fortunately the Bastard family – Thomas and his sons John and William, excellent architects and builders – were there to create a new town.

Civic dignitaries, John and William, lost their own properties in the conflagration which started in a tallow maker's shop and spread to Blandford St Mary, west of the bridge across the river Stour.

They were backed by money which had flowed in from all over the country which included £1,000 from King George II. The church they built was a great favourite with the late John Betjeman. They followed with the Town Hall, Grammar School and many houses, some unchanged today.

Blandford grew up as an important crossing place of the river Stour and, by 1305, it was important enough to have two Members of Parliament.

It is best to park in the large car park near the Stour and just wander around this Georgian town. You will find the Bastard brothers' houses next to each other. Thoughtfully, they built an ornate town pump very near them.

A cock crowing after mid-day is an ill-omen.
Dorset saying

Sherborne

Sherborne is spared great hordes of holidaymakers because it is an outpost, only four miles from Yeovil and Somerset. Those who do come though, are rewarded by seeing one of England's most attractive towns.

A place of great dignity, its Abbey was founded in 705 AD and is famous for its glorious fan vaulting. The building has been restored over the centuries but still has some original Saxon work.

Sherborne also has a public school. It was endowed as a grammar school in 1550, but there had been a school there since 705 AD when St Aldhelm was Bishop.

The school is now north of the Abbey and some of the former monastic buildings are incorporated into the modern part.

A feature of this little town of narrow streets and ancient buildings, is the yellow stone from which it is built. It glows warm on a sunny day.

Above the town are two castles. One a ruin, and a more modern edifice built by Sir Walter Raleigh as a hunting lodge in 1594. It is now the home of the Digby family.

> The moon has passed to the panes of the
>   south-aisle wall,
> And brought the mullioned shades and shines
>   to fall
> On the cheeks of a woman and man in a pew
>   there, pressed
> Together as they pant, and recline for rest.
>   *Thomas Hardy*

Sturminster Mill

Sturminster Newton is a lovely Minster town cut in two by the gently flowing Stour, Dorset's largest river. On its journey to the sea at Christchurch, the Stour waters several mills – many of them immortalised in the writings of the Rev. William Barnes, Dorset's second poet, who missed universal greatness because he chose to write much of his verse in dialect. He was born a mile or two north of this mill at Sturminster, in a cottage near Bagber, so first knowledge of his beloved Stour was gained at Hinton St Mary. He loved the river's simplicity and wrote extensively about the clote, a yellow water lily, which grows profusely on the Stour.

The bridge over the river still bears a plaque threatening transportation if wilfully damaged, and leads to the little Minster town – once the capital of the Blackmoor Vale. Now it resembles a proud old lady who has fallen on hard times. Shops, inns and houses, grouped in and around the Square, seem to miss the bustle of 19th-century days when Sturminster was an important industrial centre. Now it is the home of some of Dorset's kindest and proudest folk. They will smile and pass the time of day with strangers, and there is always laughter as shopkeepers gossip with the customers. In the evenings some of the older ones still meet and read aloud the works of William Barnes.

Be there any leaves to quiver
On the Aspen by the river?
Doo he sheade the water still,
Where the rushes be a growen,
Where the sullen Stours a-flowen
Drough the meads vrom mill to mill?
Vor if a tree were dear to me,
Oh! 'twer thik aspen by the river.
William Barnes

Wimborne

Wimborne resembles a cathedral city in miniature, but leading historians find little to muse about when writing of this Minster town on the banks of the twisting Stour. Said Sir Frederick Treves, 'a commonplace town squatting soberly in the meadows. There is little to show that it ever had been – as Leland avers – "a very large thing". It is a characterless place, that having set its face against any show of individuality, has become successfully mediocre.'

Treves agrees that it is best viewed from afar and this view across the Stour's water meadows is a daily picture for those who motor along the new bypass.

The unique Minster has two towers, one a glorious lantern tower of the late Norman period, and a western tower dating from the 15th century. Its rich colours are the main attraction. Many different stones were used in the construction. The western tower is a column of green and grey, but the Norman tower glows with red Ringwood sandstone.

Visitors pause before entering the Norman Nave to see and hear the Quarter Jack strike out the time. Today the figure is carved out of wood and crudely painted in the uniform of a 19th century Grenadier but, when first made in the 17th century, the striker wore the garb of a monk.

The Minster displays the burial place of Anthony Ettrick, a Recorder of Poole, who declared he would neither lie inside nor outside the church. His stone coffin stands in a niche in the wall, neither underground nor overground, neither in nor out. He died in 1703.

Dry our eyes in weeping,
Shut our eyes in sleeping.
William Barnes on
his deathbed

River Stour

The rustic Stour rises beyond the county boundary and twists like a writhing snake through the Dorset valleys, turning the wheels of the mills which are dotted along its untidy banks; gently flowing as if not wanting to disturb the yellow clote which grows profusely 'neath its banks.

It proudly offers facilities for the oarsmen of two public schools, and adds beauty to the Minster towns which grew up on its banks. Then, swollen in size by several tributaries, it prepares to enter the heavily populated coastal towns of Bournemouth and Christchurch, where authority has trimmed the banks and straightened the bends to make it tidy and in keeping with the urban area.

One of the river's last displays of beauty is at Parley where beneath the heights of Dudsbury, first fortified by men of the Iron Age, the bare trees cloak themselves in shimmering frost and reflect in the blue water.

Peaceful now, it can forget the day in 52 AD when Romans under Vespasian came along the river and took Dudsbury by storm.

Still glides the stream and shall forever glide;
The Form remains, the Function never dies.
Wordsworth

Blandford Avenue

The farmer who planted the trees which line two miles of the road between Wimborne and Blandford, alongside the ramparts of Badbury Rings, is said to have planted one for each day of the year. But if you care to count, you will find over 365 trees on one side alone.

Beautiful at all times of the year, in summer the leaves and branches meet and form a giant cathedral-like nave with the rounded tree trunks analogous to sturdy Norman pillars. In winter, as seen here, the sun makes beautiful patterns and reflects warm colours off the rotting autumn leaves.

Countless lovers have carved their marks on the smooth bark of the trees, and we are left wondering whether GF meant what he said to EL in 1928, or whether AT and BG encased in a carved heart are still that way.

One thing is certain . . . for all those who have dallied here the record that they once loved is preserved here, perhaps for centuries.

Here in the avenue
Raking up leaves,
Lords and ladies pass in view,
Until one heaves
Sighs at life's russet hue,
Raking up leaves.
Thomas Hardy

Acknowledgements

My thanks to Brian Galpin, a stalwart Man of Poole, who lent his collection of Dorset sayings, and to Di Prestell who so patiently typed my untidy manuscript.

I am grateful to Southern Newspapers PLC for allowing my photographs taken for the Echo calendar to be used in this book, and also to David Golumb for his photograph of Maiden Castle.

Finally I would like to thank Nicholas Battle of Countryside Books who made the final selection of photographs from hundreds of transparencies.
Harry Ashley

The photographs in this book, taken by the author, are reproduced by kind permission of the Evening Echo, Bournemouth.

Bibliography

William Barnes, 'Poems of Rural Life in the Dorset Dialect', Kegan Paul, Trubner & Co.
Thomas Hardy, 'Thomas Hardy Complete Poems', Macmillan.